To Celebrate

Date

THANK YOU FOR COMING.

Let's celebrate!

Guest Name

Wishes & Messages

Email/Phone

Guest Name

Wishes & Messages

EMAIL/PHONE

Guest Name

Wishes & Messages

Email/Phone

Guest Name

Wishes & Messages

Email/Phone

Guest Name
Wishes & Messages
Email/Phone

Guest Name

Wishes & Messages

Email/Phone

Guest Name
Wishes & Messages
Email/Phone

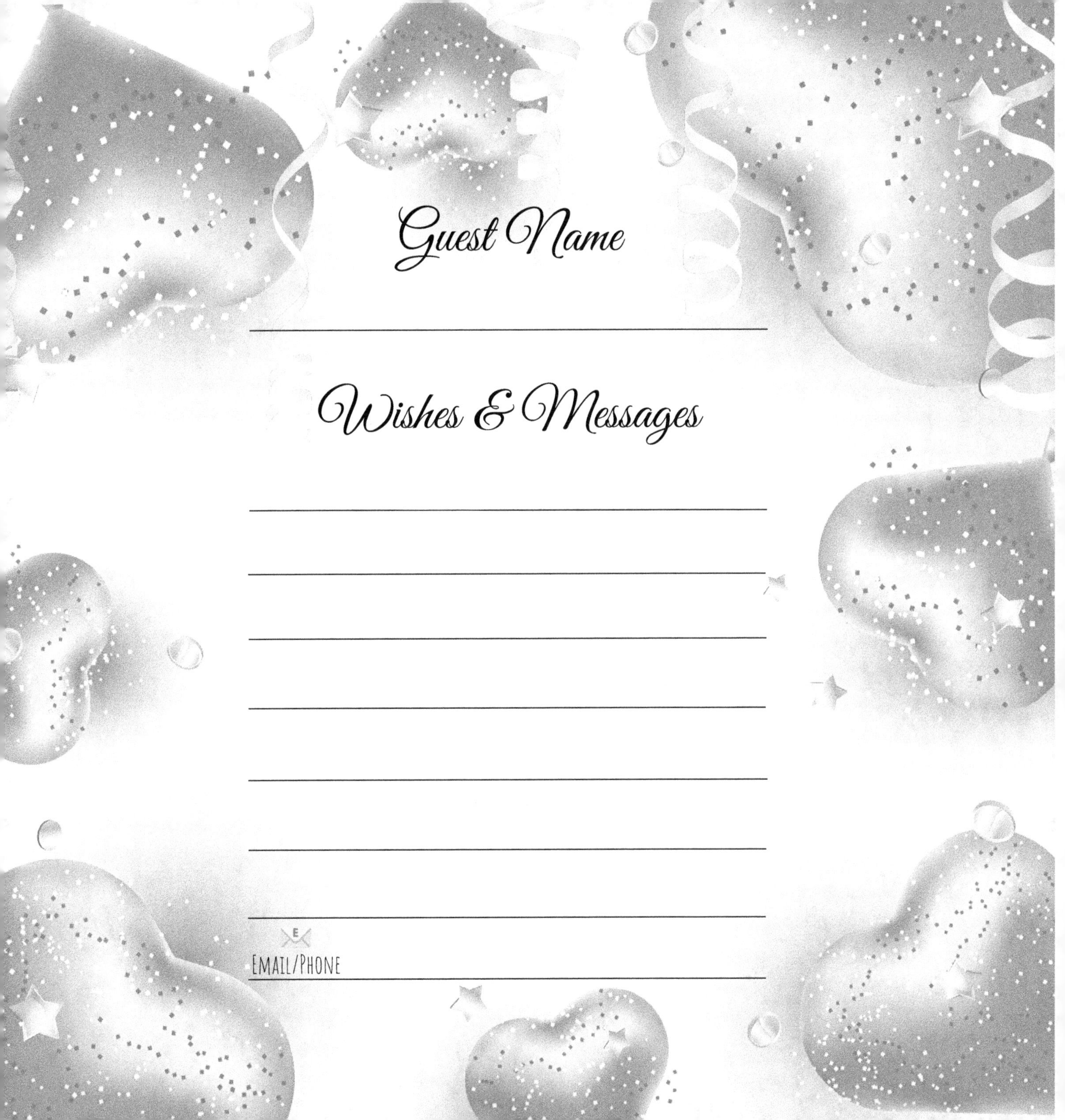

Guest Name

Wishes & Messages

Email/Phone

Guest Name

____

Wishes & Messages

____

____

____

____

____

____
Email/Phone
____

Guest Name
Wishes & Messages
Email/Phone

Guest Name
Wishes & Messages
Email/Phone

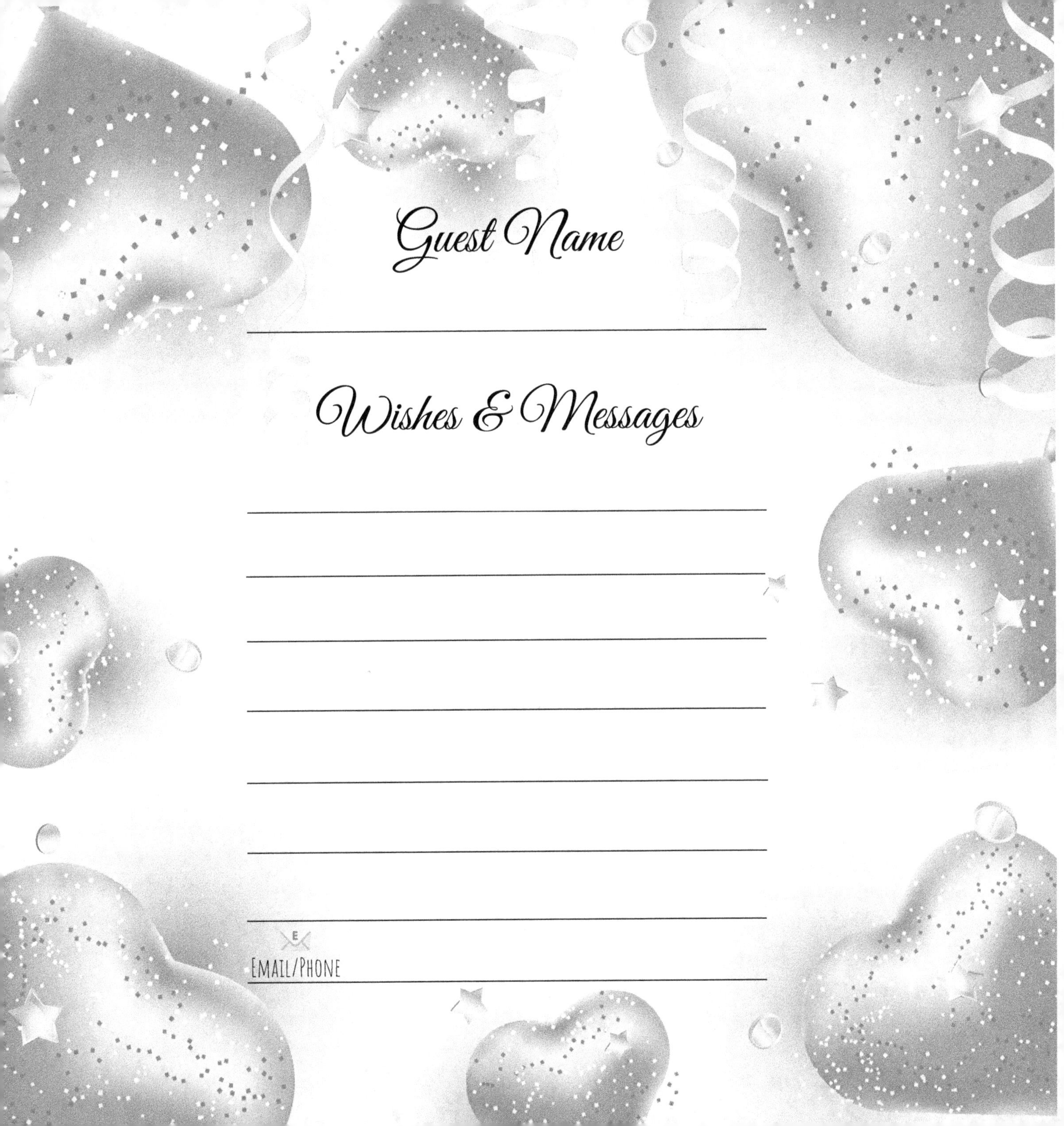

Guest Name
Wishes & Messages
Email/Phone

Guest Name
Wishes & Messages
Email/Phone

Guest Name
Wishes & Messages
Email/Phone

Guest Name
Wishes & Messages
Email/Phone

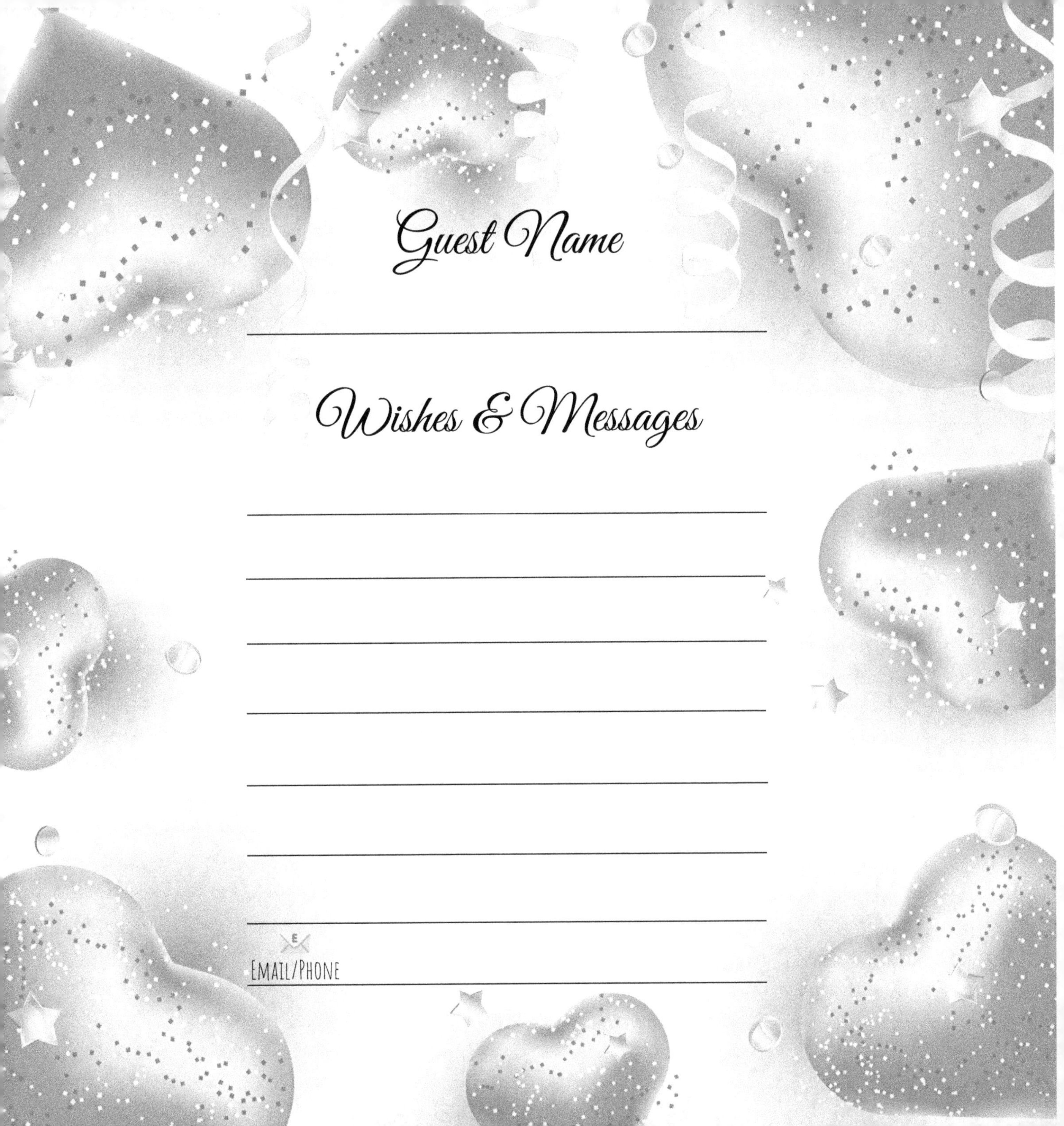

Guest Name

Wishes & Messages

Email/Phone

Guest Name

Wishes & Messages

Email/Phone

Guest Name
Wishes & Messages
Email/Phone

Guest Name
Wishes & Messages
Email/Phone

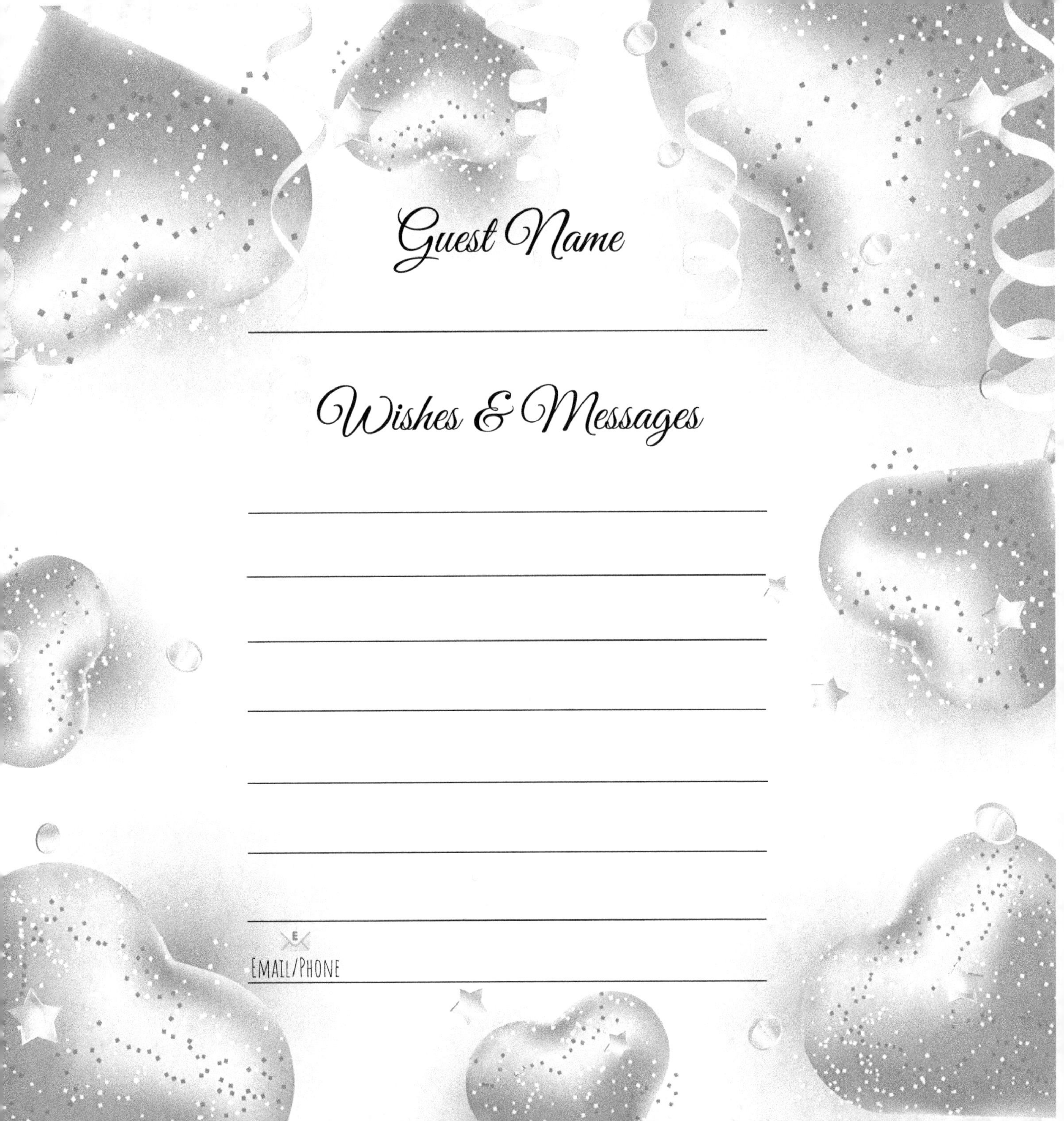

Guest Name
Wishes & Messages
Email/Phone

Guest Name

Wishes & Messages

Email/Phone

Guest Name
Wishes & Messages
Email/Phone

Guest Name
Wishes & Messages
Email/Phone

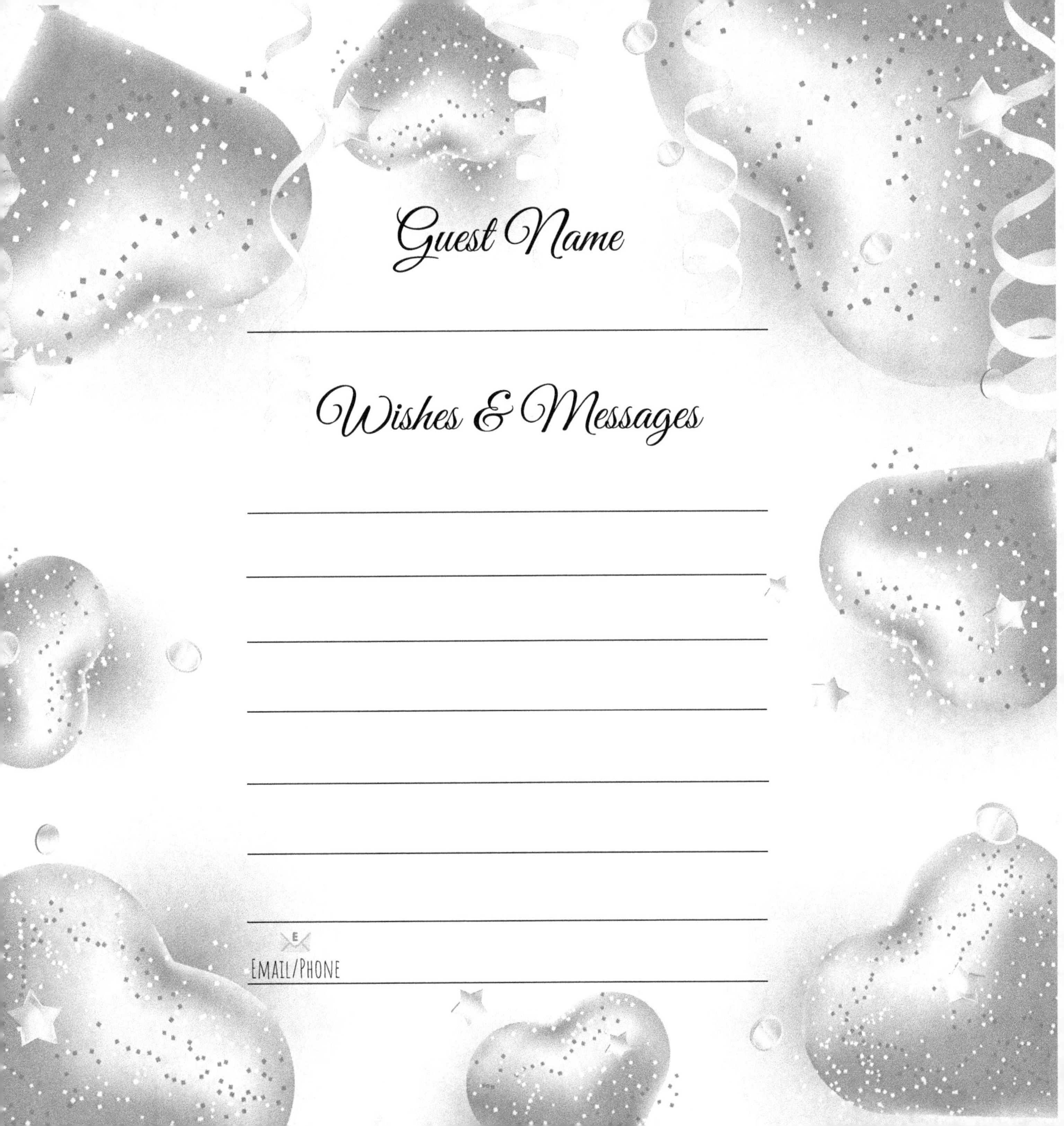

Guest Name
Wishes & Messages
Email/Phone

Guest Name

Wishes & Messages

Email/Phone

Guest Name
Wishes & Messages
Email/Phone

Guest Name

Wishes & Messages

Email/Phone

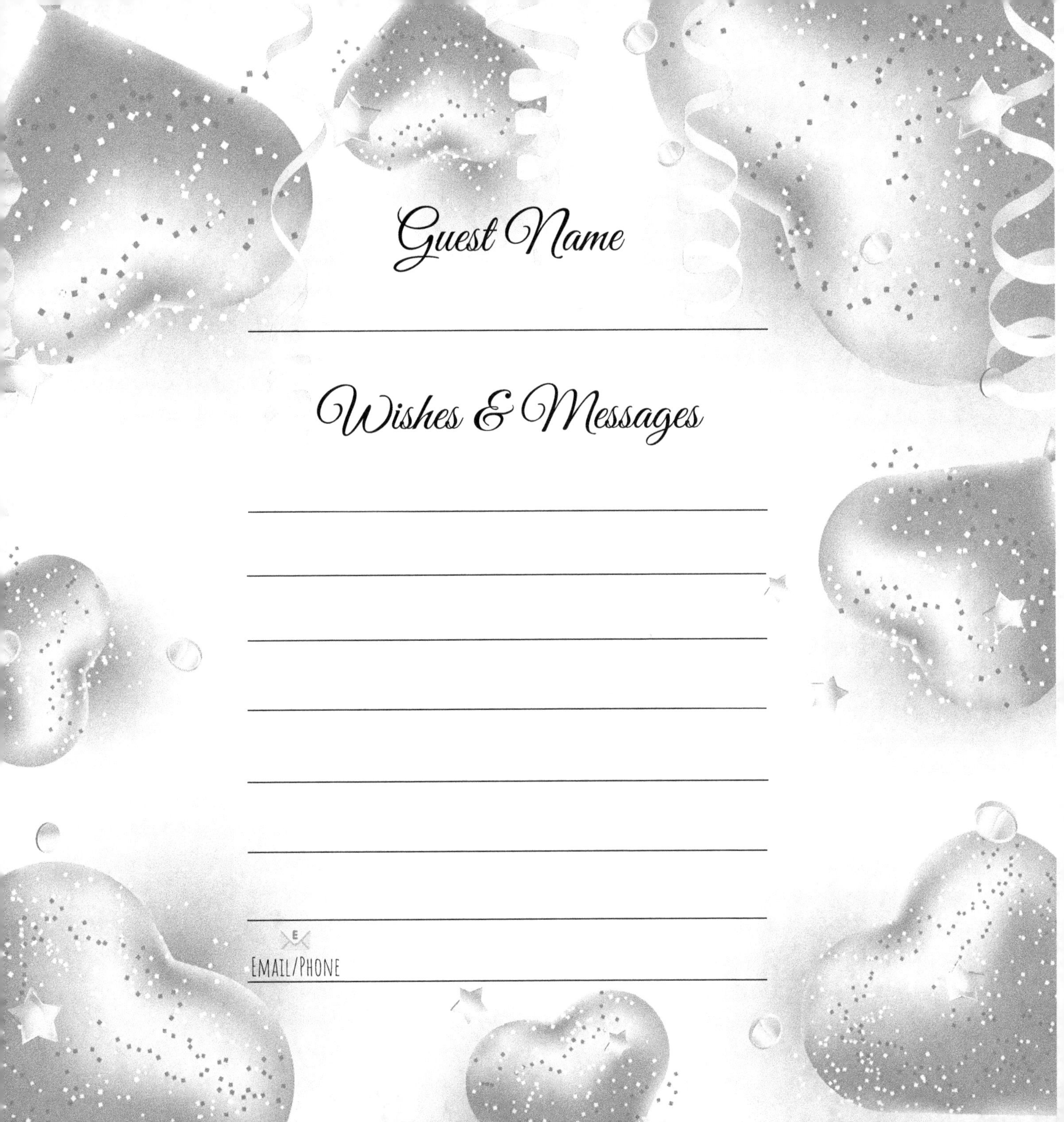
Guest Name

Wishes & Messages

Email/Phone

Guest Name
Wishes & Messages
Email/Phone

Guest Name
Wishes & Messages
Email/Phone

Guest Name

Wishes & Messages

Email/Phone

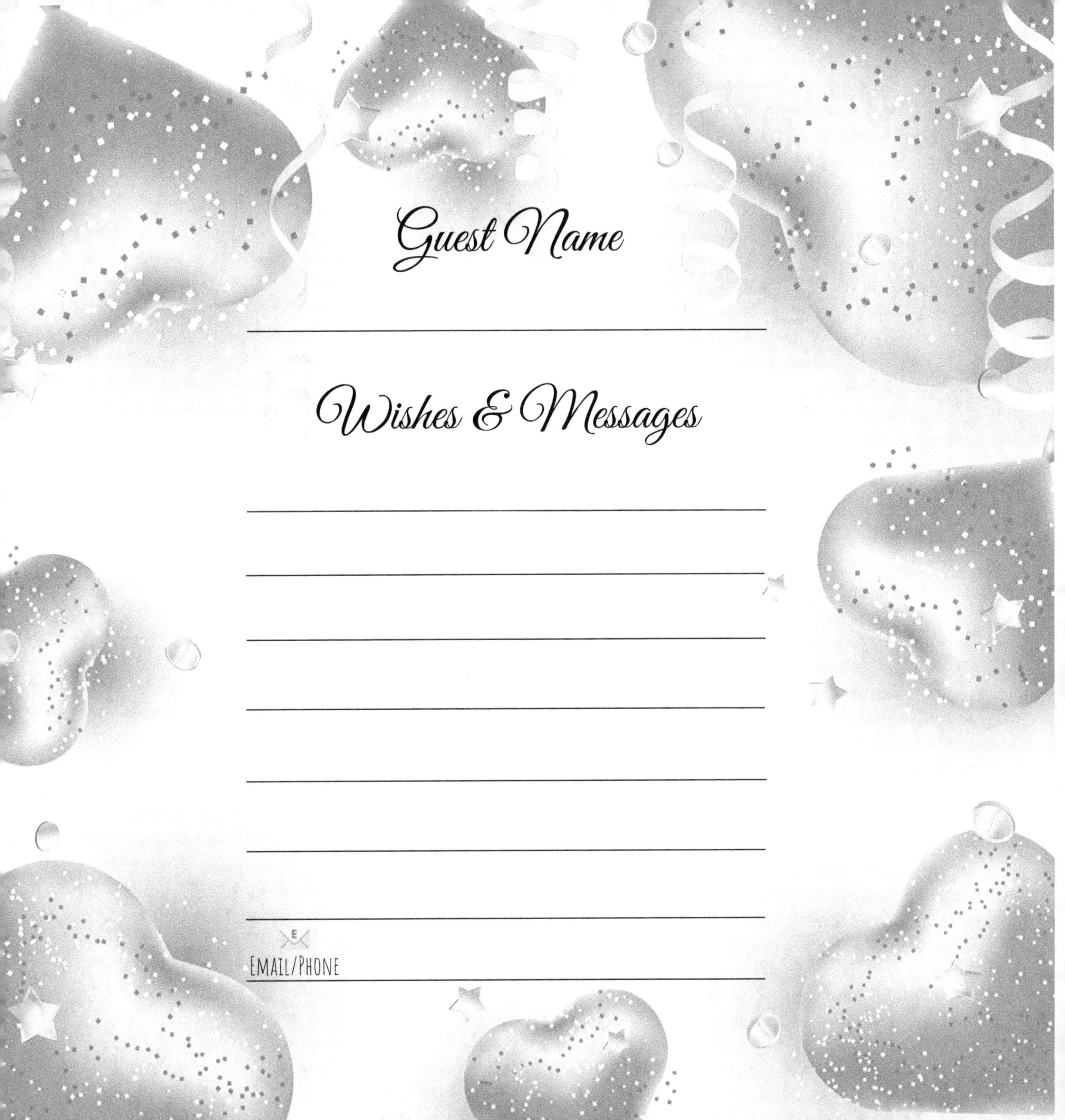

Guest Name
Wishes & Messages
Email/Phone

Guest Name
Wishes & Messages
Email/Phone

Guest Name

Wishes & Messages

Email/Phone

Guest Name

Wishes & Messages

Email/Phone

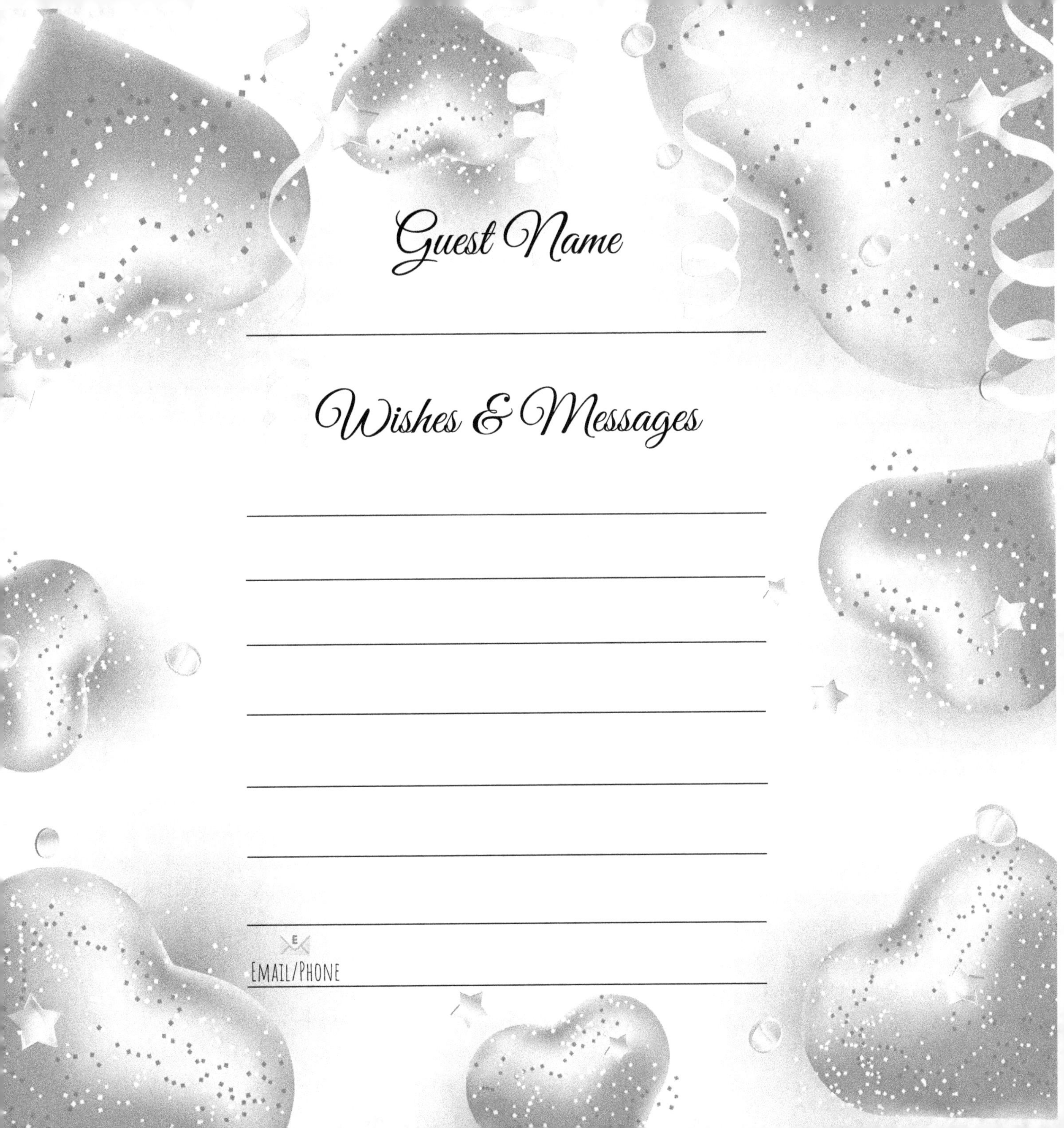

Guest Name

Wishes & Messages

Email/Phone

Guest Name

Wishes & Messages

Email/Phone

Guest Name

Wishes & Messages

Email/Phone

Guest Name
Wishes & Messages
Email/Phone

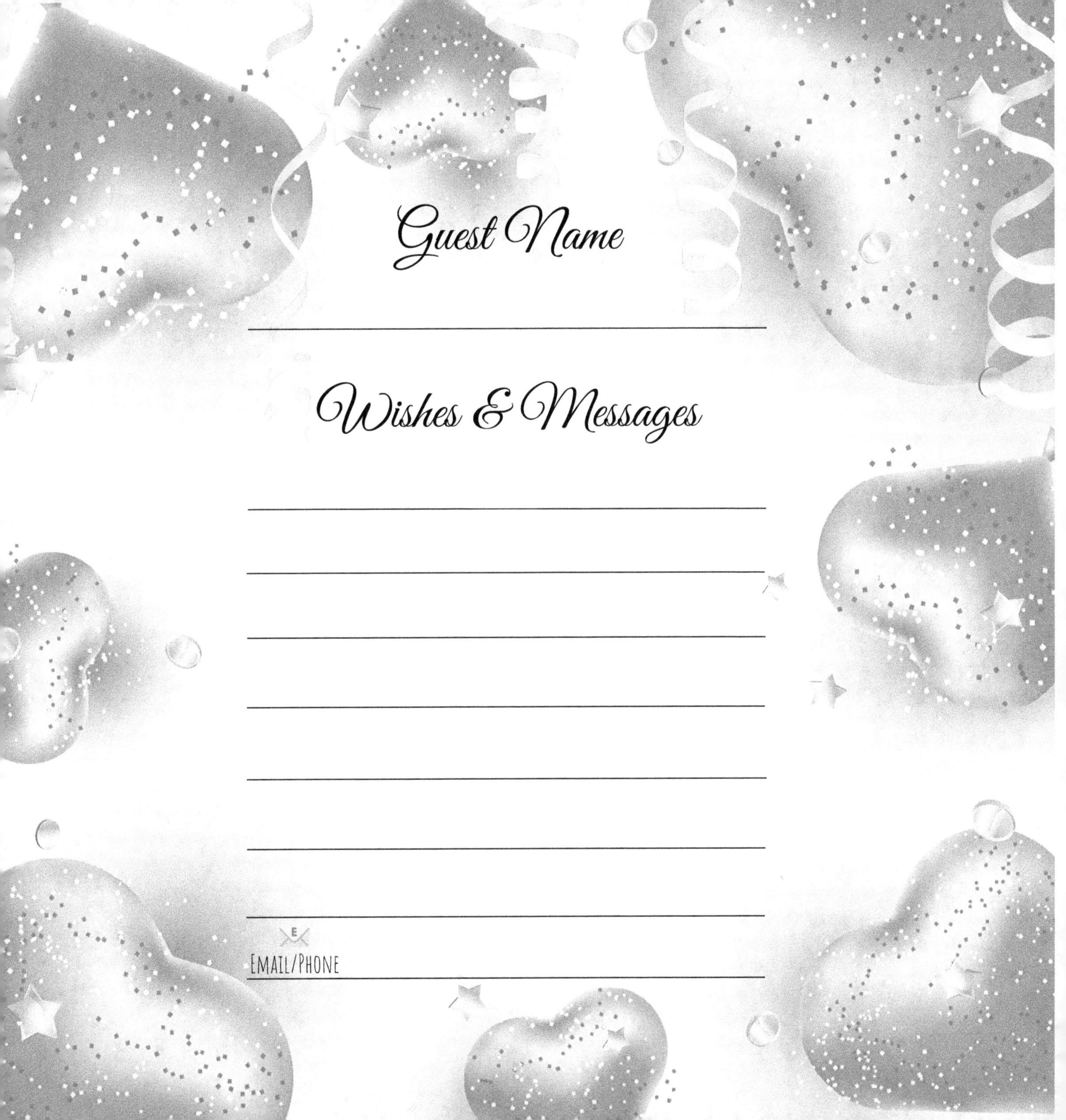

Guest Name

Wishes & Messages

Email/Phone

Guest Name

Wishes & Messages

Email/Phone

Guest Name
Wishes & Messages
Email/Phone

Guest Name

Wishes & Messages

Email/Phone

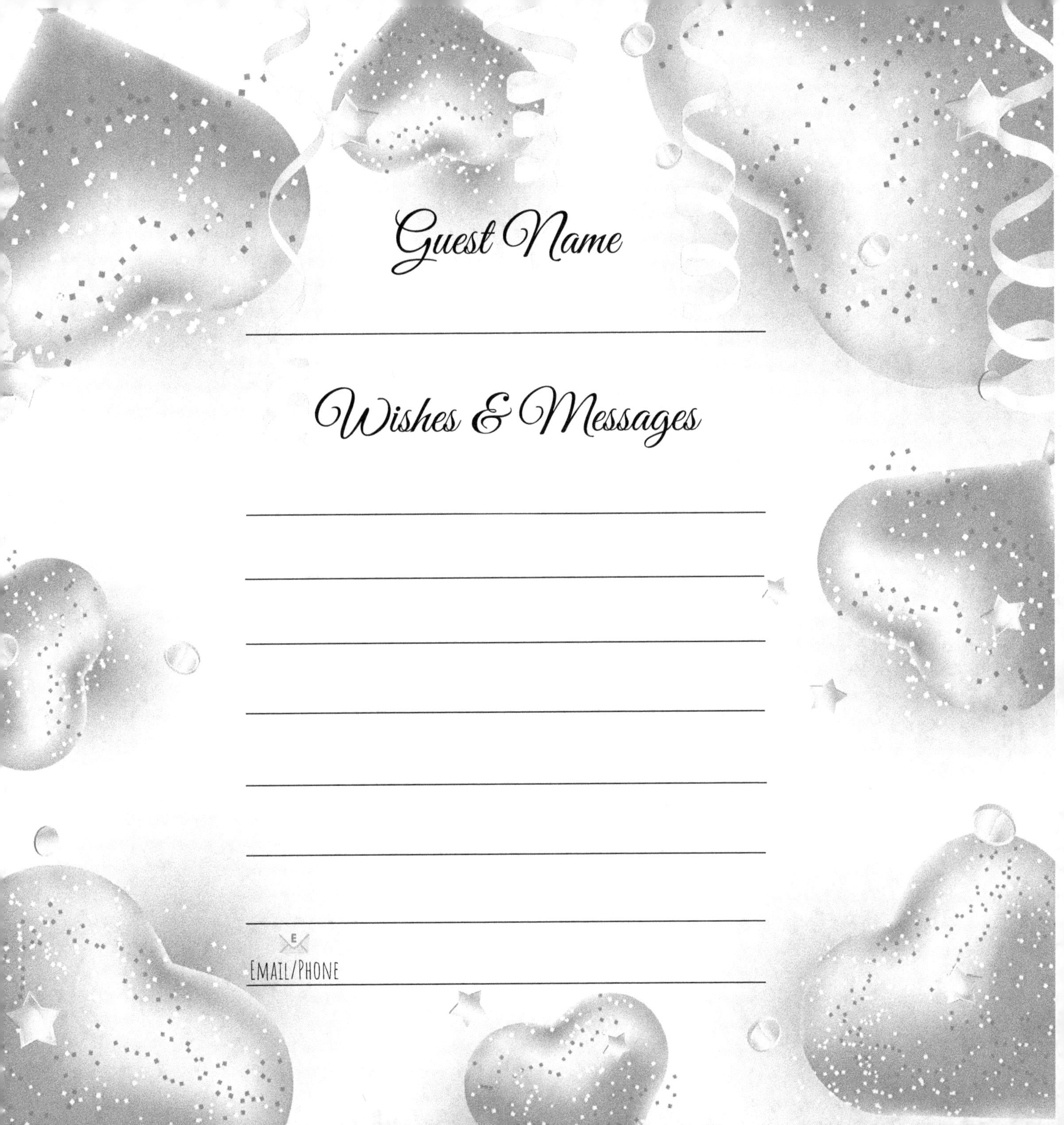

Guest Name
Wishes & Messages
Email/Phone

Guest Name

Wishes & Messages

Email/Phone

Guest Name
Wishes & Messages
Email/Phone

Guest Name
Wishes & Messages
Email/Phone

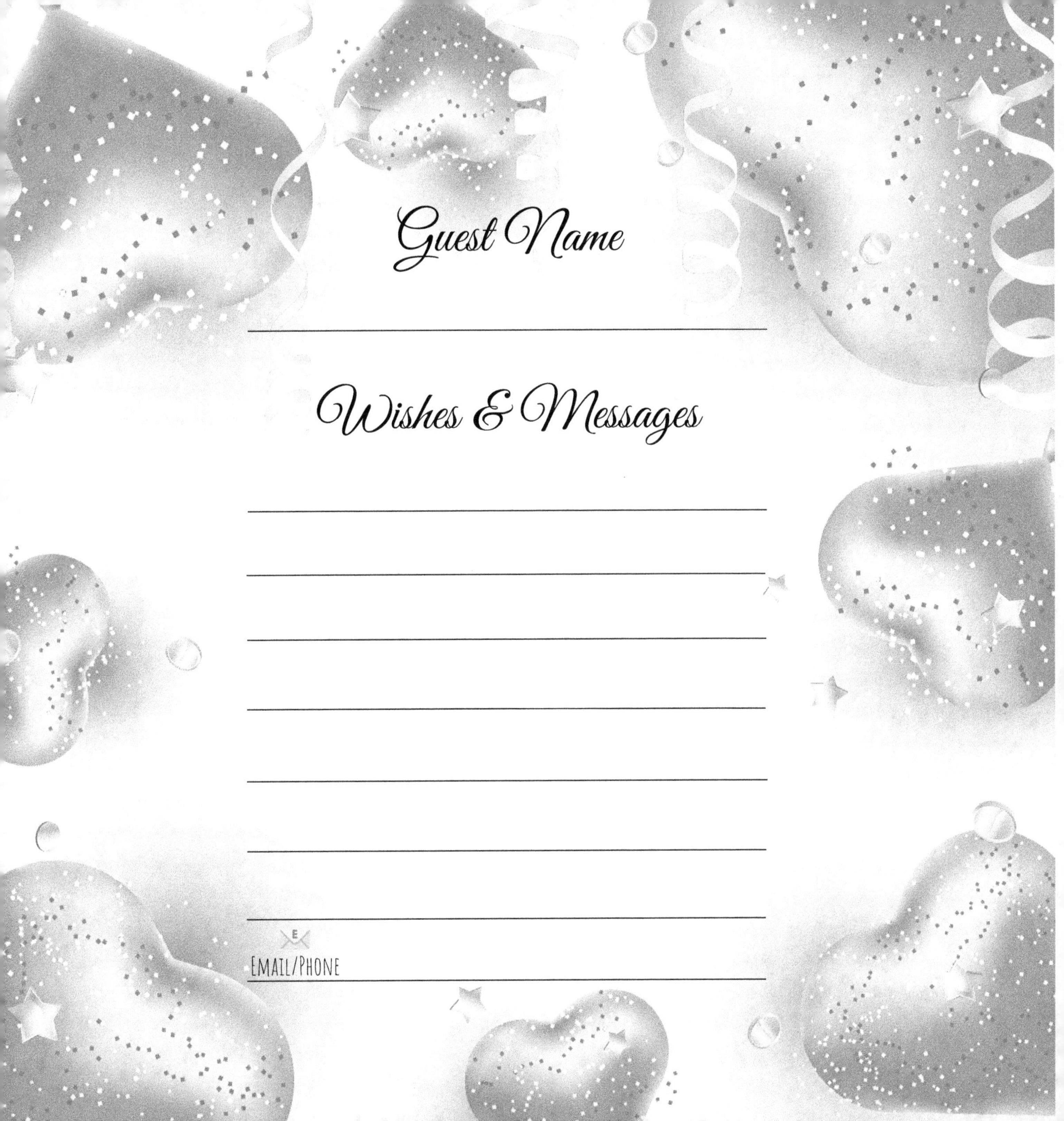

Guest Name

Wishes & Messages

E
Email/Phone

Guest Name
Wishes & Messages
Email/Phone

Guest Name

Wishes & Messages

Email/Phone

Guest Name

Wishes & Messages

Email/Phone

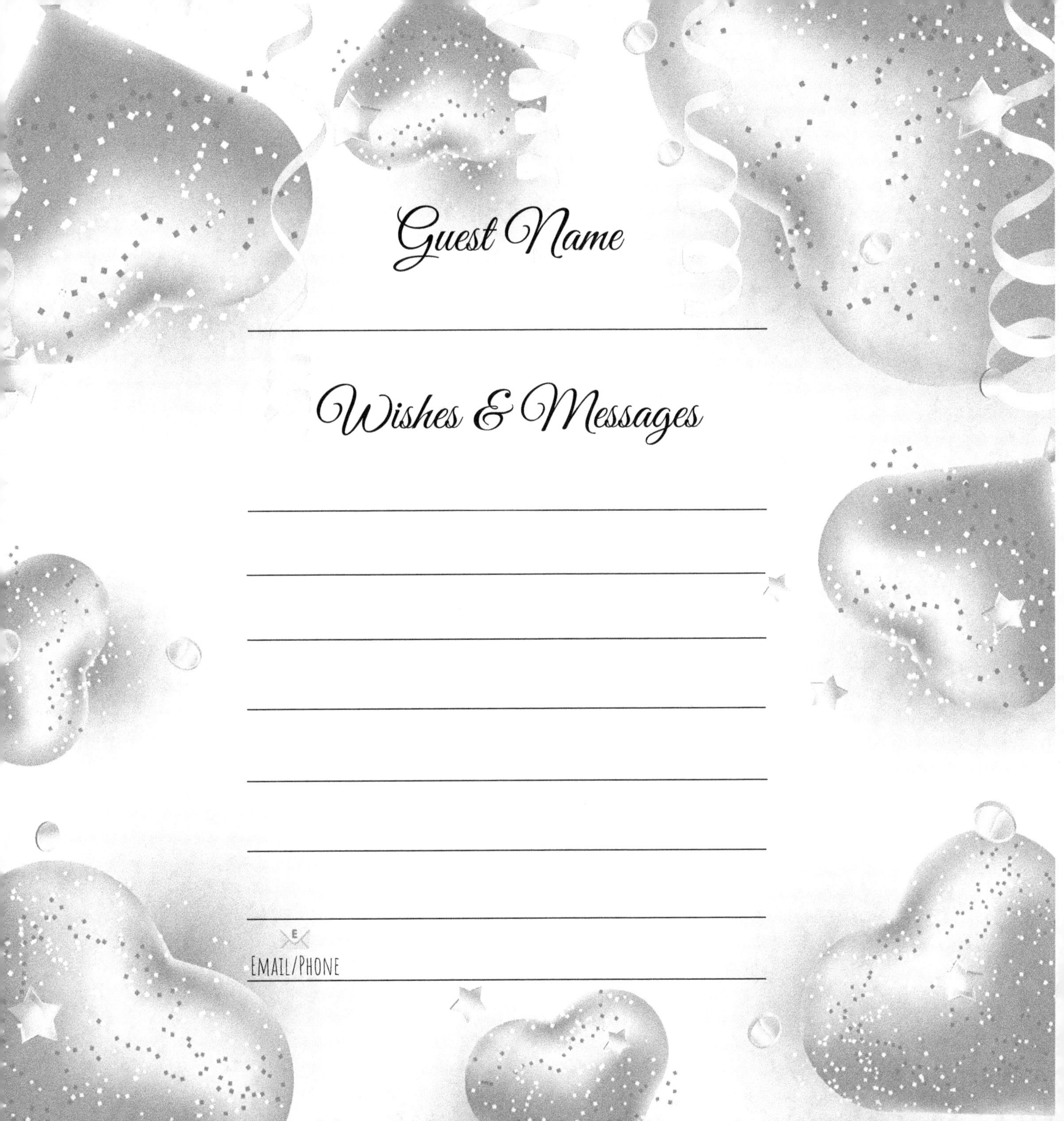

Guest Name

Wishes & Messages

Email/Phone

Guest Name

Wishes & Messages

Email/Phone

Guest Name
Wishes & Messages
Email/Phone

Guest Name
Wishes & Messages
Email/Phone

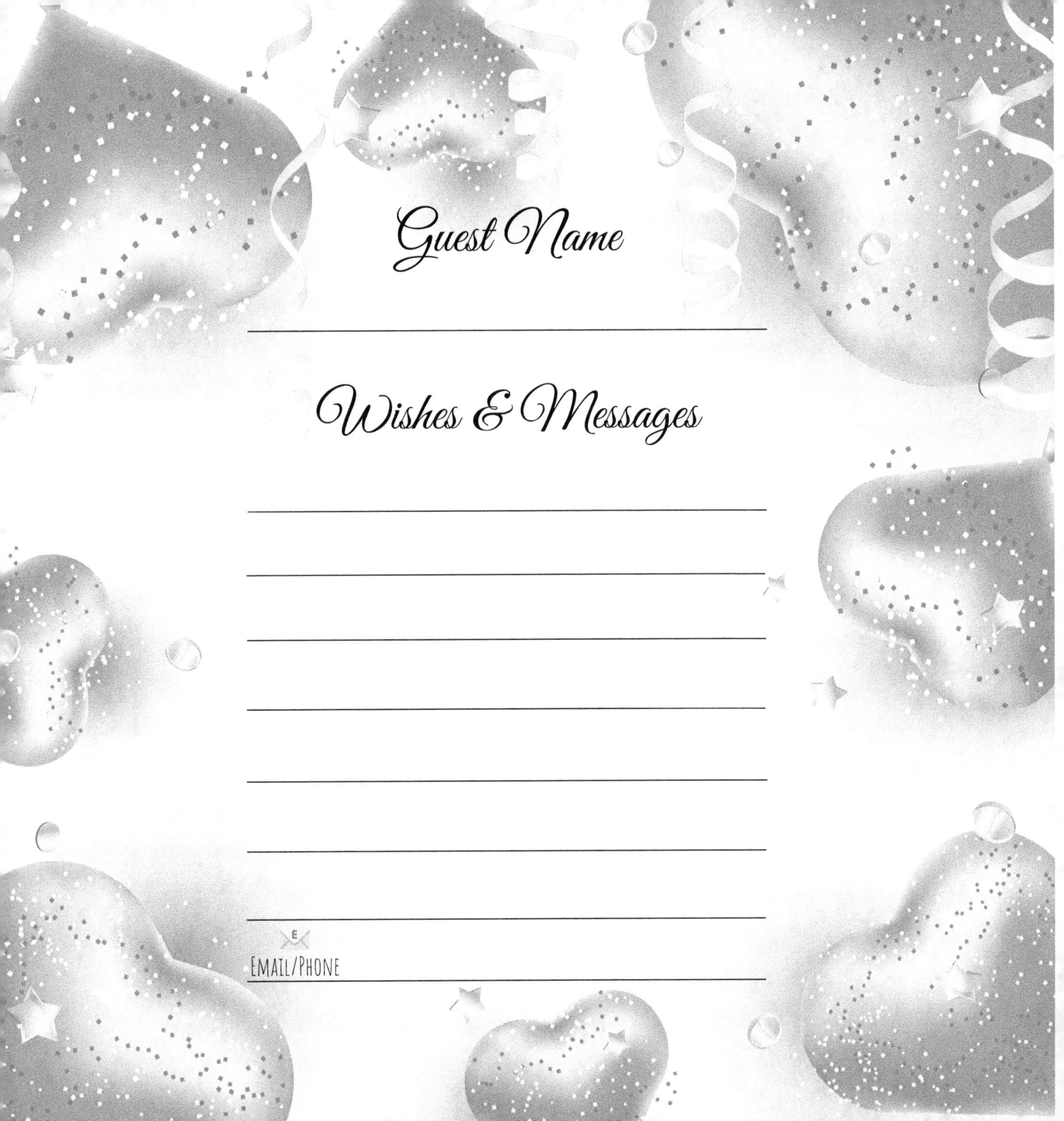

Guest Name

Wishes & Messages

Email/Phone

Guest Name
Wishes & Messages
Email/Phone

Guest Name

Wishes & Messages

Email/Phone

Guest Name

Wishes & Messages

Email/Phone

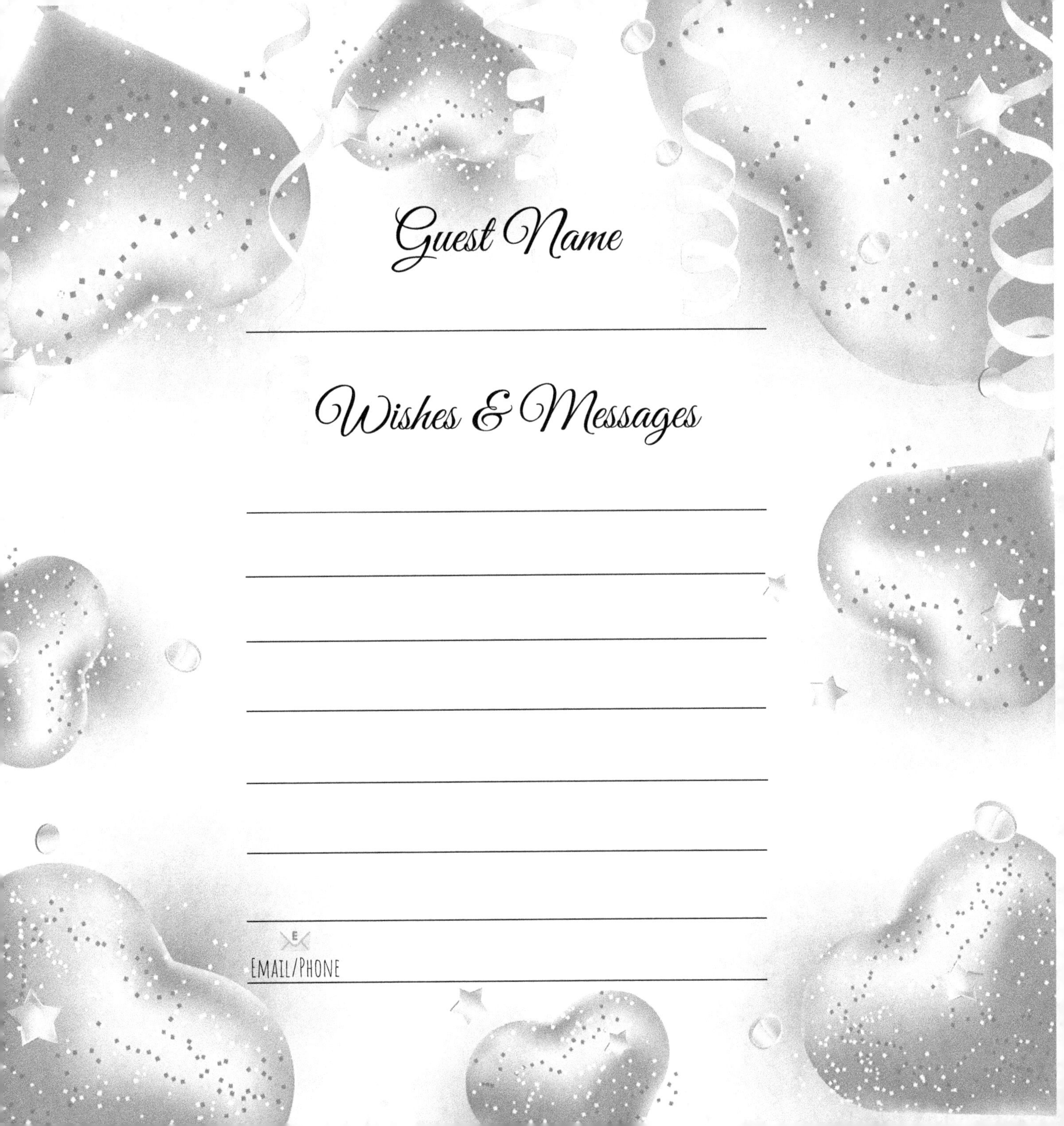

Guest Name

____

Wishes & Messages

____

____

____

____

____

Email/Phone
____

Guest Name

Wishes & Messages

Email/Phone

Guest Name

Wishes & Messages

Email/Phone

Guest Name

Wishes & Messages

Email/Phone

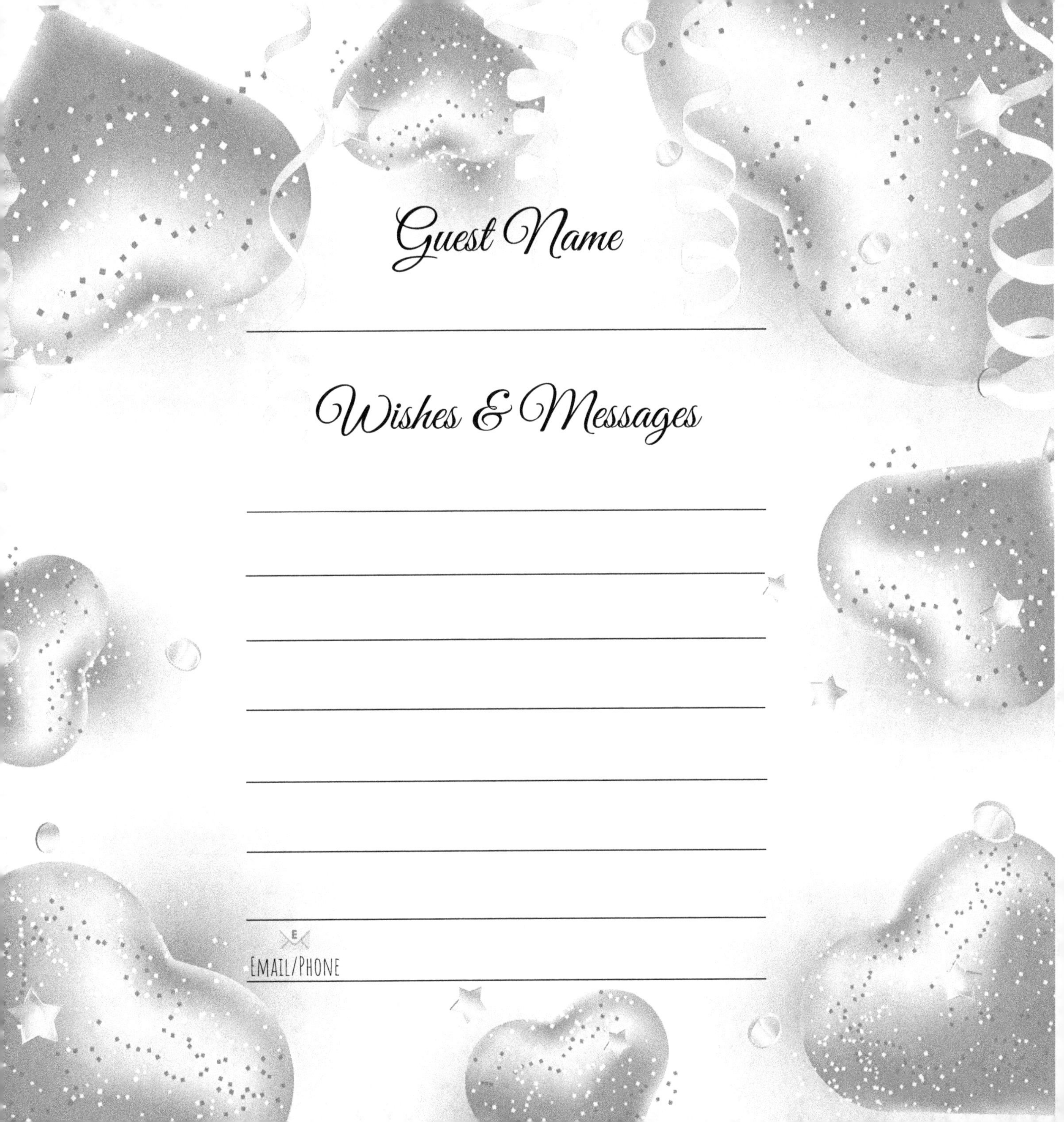

Guest Name
Wishes & Messages
Email/Phone

Guest Name
Wishes & Messages
Email/Phone

# Guest Name

Wishes & Messages

Email/Phone

Guest Name
Wishes & Messages
Email/Phone

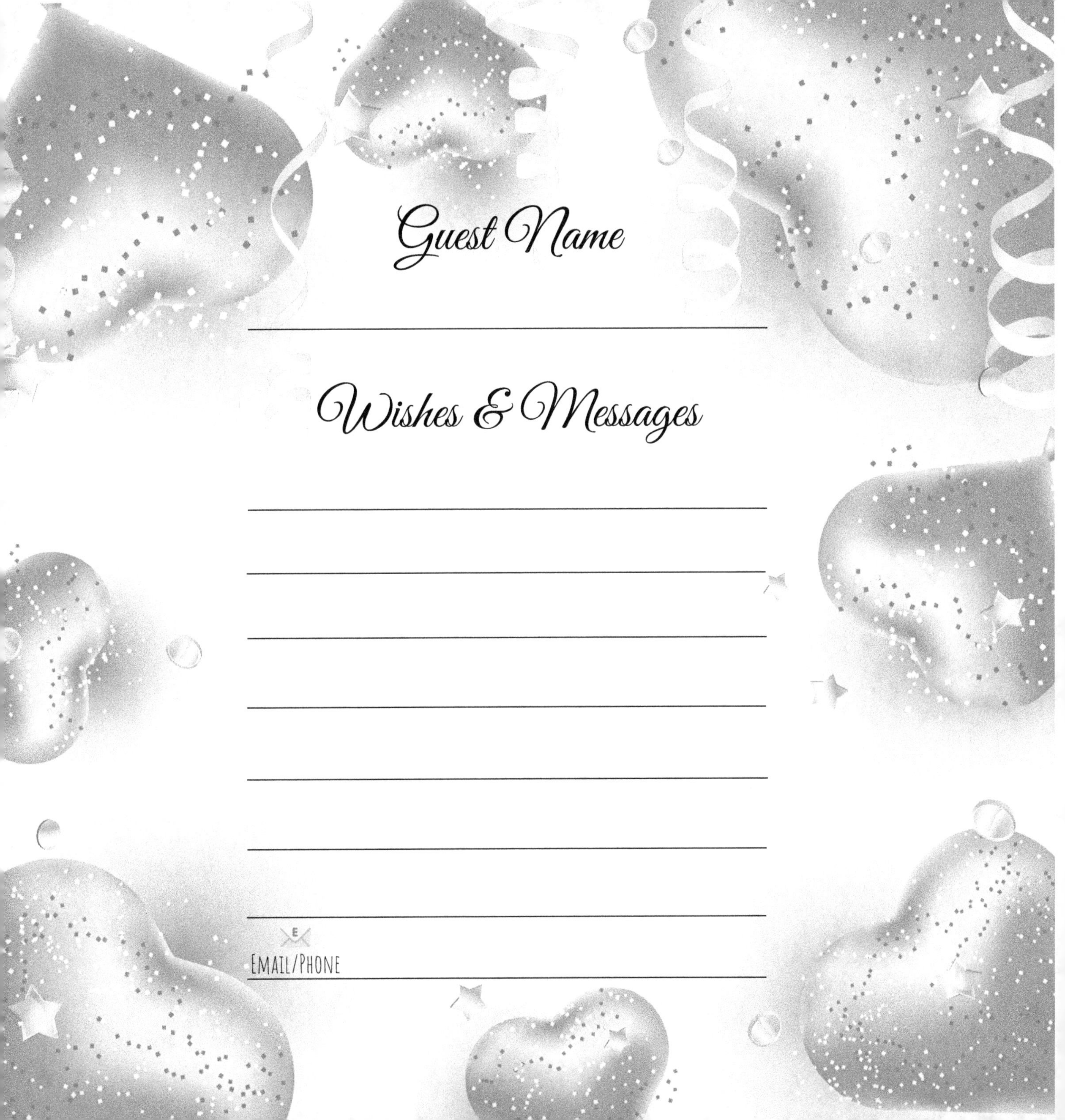

Guest Name

Wishes & Messages

Email/Phone

Guest Name
Wishes & Messages
Email/Phone

Guest Name

Wishes & Messages

Email/Phone

Guest Name
Wishes & Messages
Email/Phone

Guest Name

Wishes & Messages

Email/Phone

Guest Name

Wishes & Messages

Email/Phone

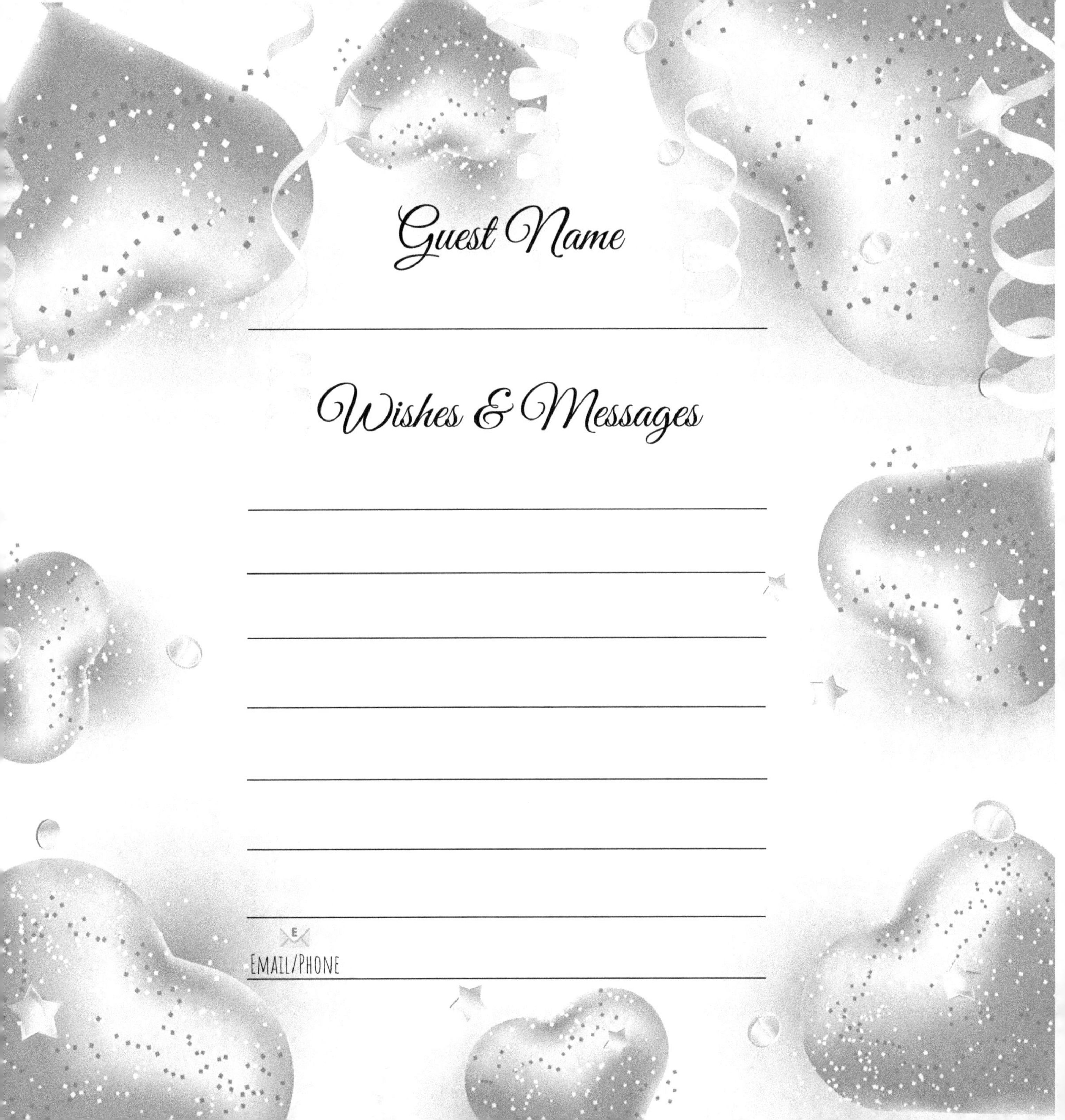

Guest Name

Wishes & Messages

Email/Phone

Guest Name

Wishes & Messages

Email/Phone

Guest Name
Wishes & Messages
Email/Phone

Guest Name

Wishes & Messages

Email/Phone

Guest Name

Wishes & Messages

Email/Phone

Guest Name
Wishes & Messages
Email/Phone

Guest Name

Wishes & Messages

Email/Phone

Guest Name

Wishes & Messages

Email/Phone

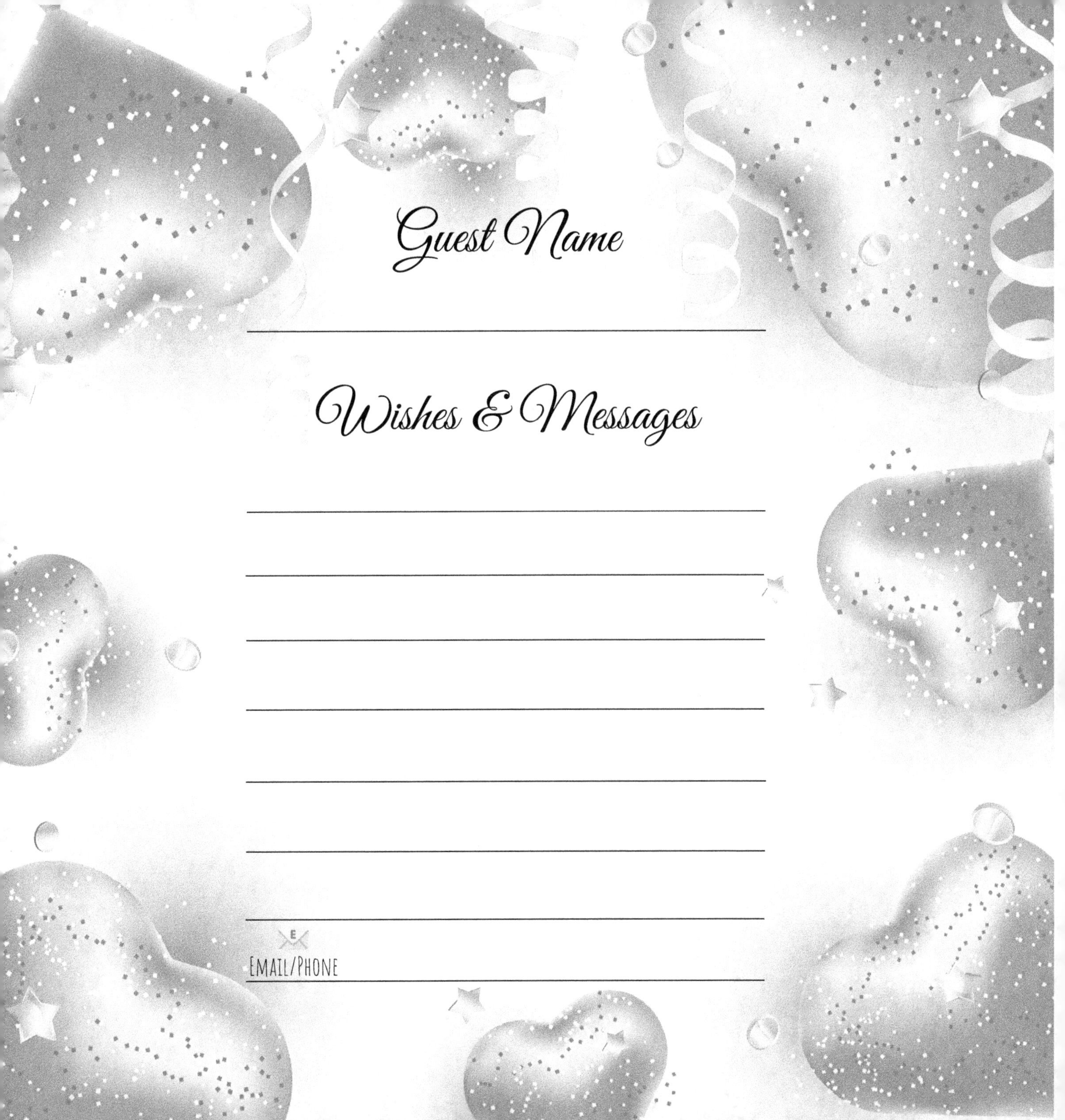

Guest Name

Wishes & Messages

Email/Phone

Guest Name

Wishes & Messages

EMAIL/PHONE

Guest Name
Wishes & Messages
Email/Phone

Guest Name

Wishes & Messages

Email/Phone

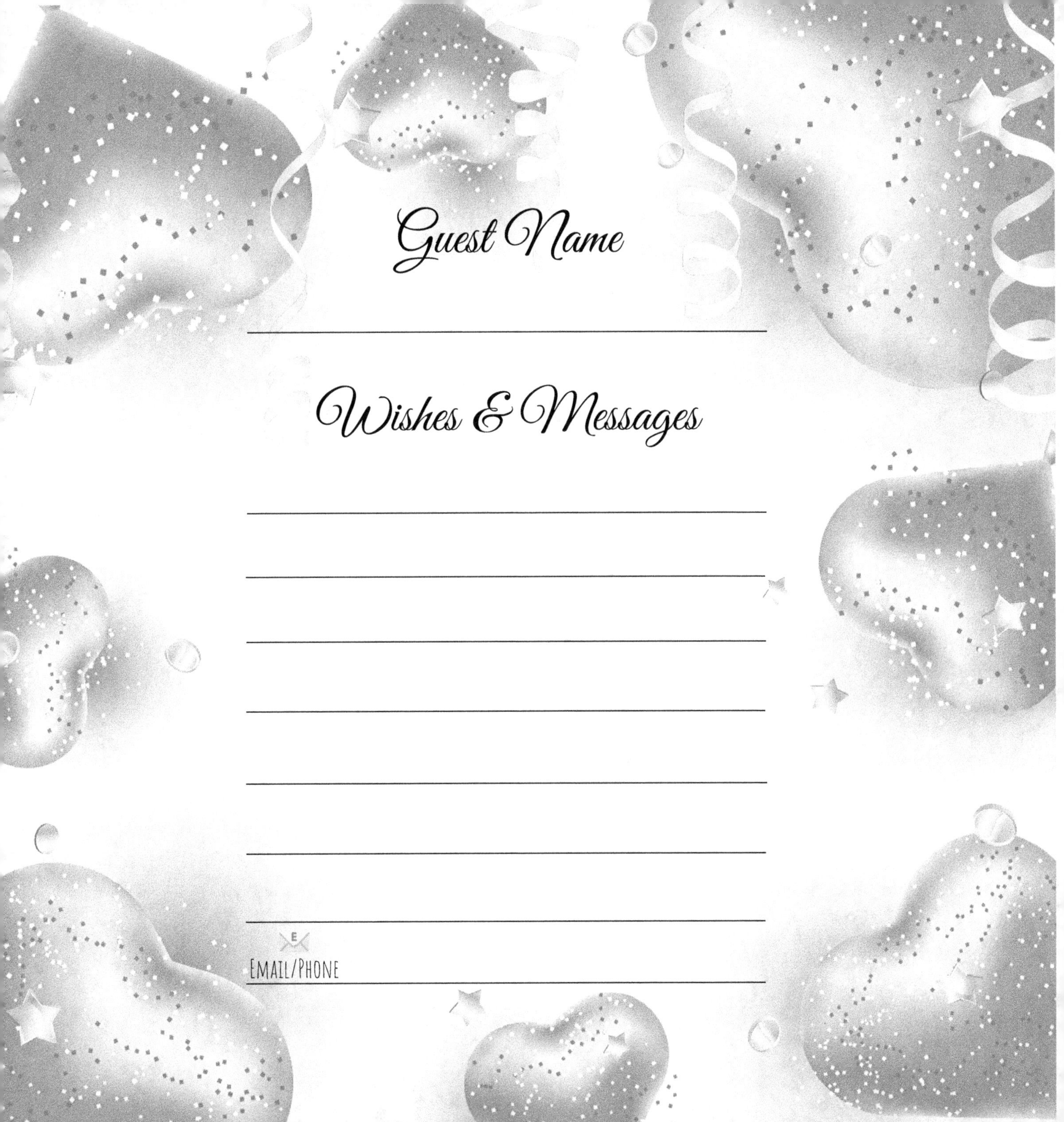Guest Name

Wishes & Messages

Email/Phone

Guest Name
Wishes & Messages
Email/Phone

Guest Name
Wishes & Messages
Email/Phone

Guest Name

Wishes & Messages

Email/Phone

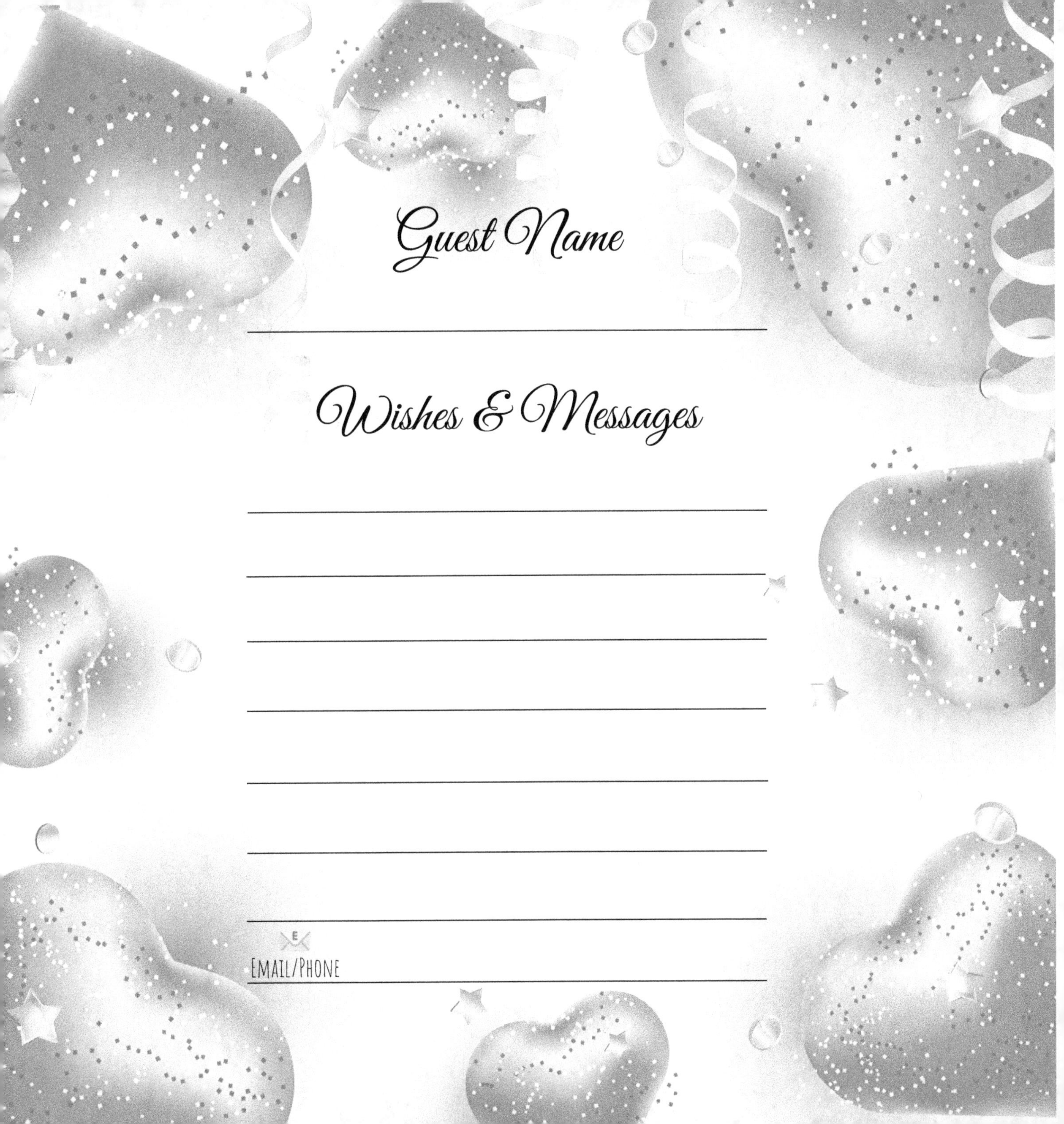
Guest Name

Wishes & Messages

Email/Phone

Guest Name

Wishes & Messages

Email/Phone

Guest Name

Wishes & Messages

Email/Phone

Guest Name

Wishes & Messages

Email/Phone

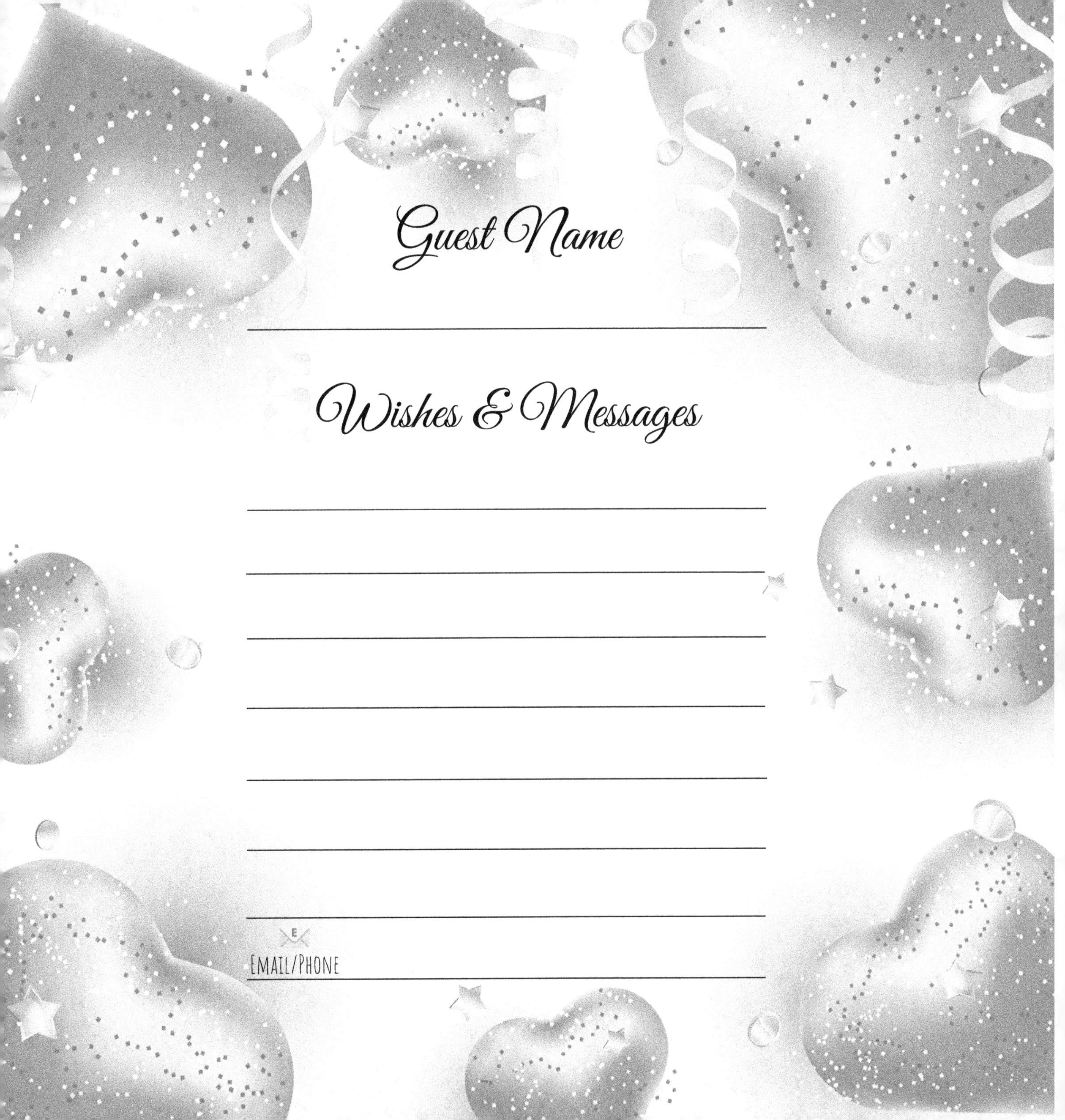

Guest Name
Wishes & Messages
Email/Phone

Guest Name
Wishes & Messages
Email/Phone

Guest Name

Wishes & Messages

Email/Phone

Guest Name

Wishes & Messages

Email/Phone

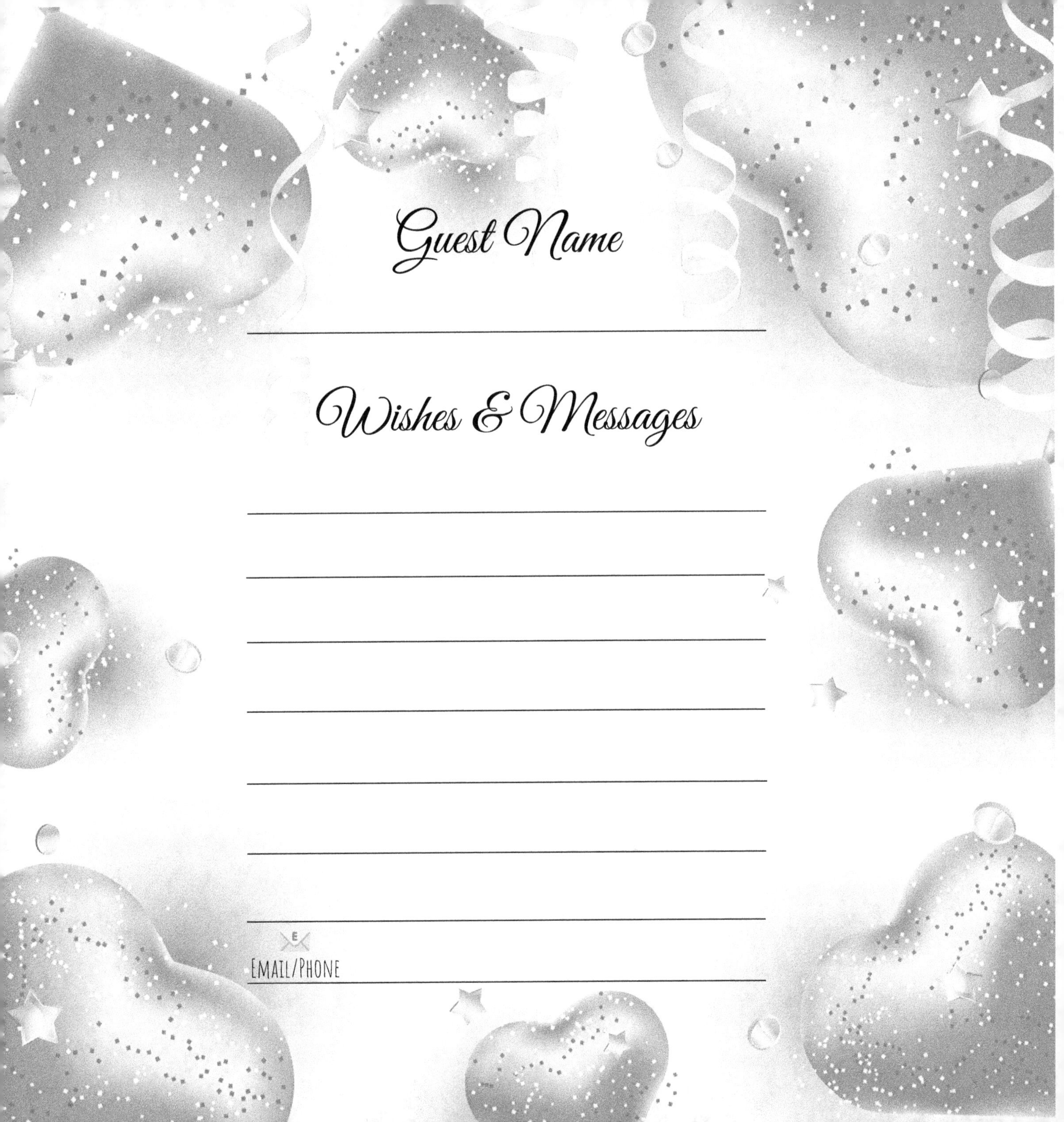

Guest Name

Wishes & Messages

Email/Phone

Guest Name

Wishes & Messages

Email/Phone

Guest Name

Wishes & Messages

Email/Phone

Guest Name
Wishes & Messages
Email/Phone

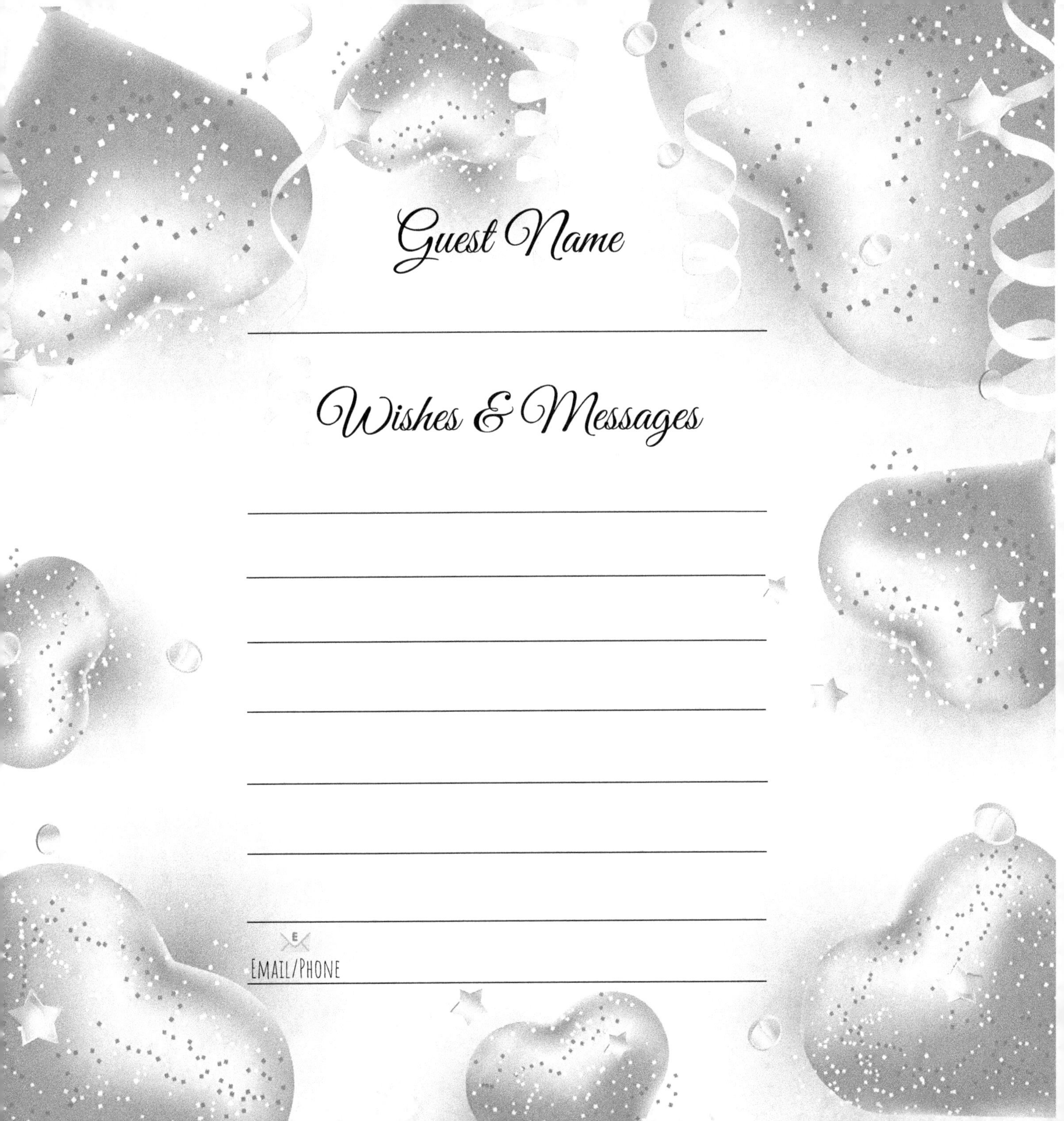

Guest Name

Wishes & Messages

Email/Phone

Guest Name

Wishes & Messages

Email/Phone

Guest Name
Wishes & Messages
Email/Phone

Guest Name

Wishes & Messages

Email/Phone

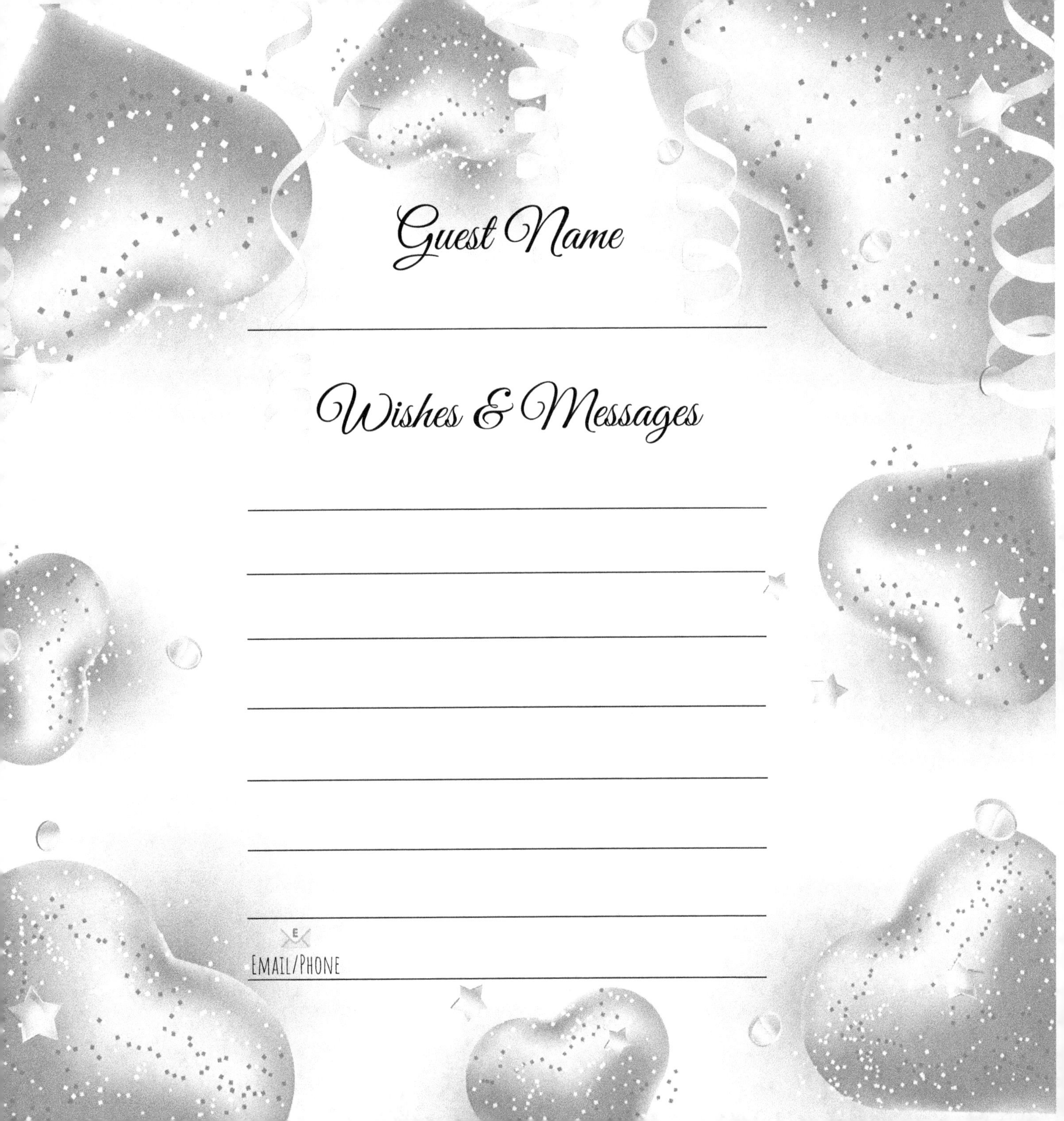

Guest Name
Wishes & Messages
Email/Phone

Guest Name

Wishes & Messages

Email/Phone

NOTES & PHOTOS

NOTES & PHOTOS

NOTES & PHOTOS

NOTES & PHOTOS

NOTES & PHOTOS

GIFT LOG

Name / Email / Phone   Gift

GIFT LOG

Name / Email / Phone	Gift

GIFT LOG

Name /Email /Phone | Gift

GIFT LOG

Name /Email /Phone

Gift

GIFT LOG

Name / Email / Phone

Gift

GIFT LOG

Name / Email / Phone   Gift

GIFT LOG

Name / Email / Phone	Gift